Table of Contents

MyPlate

The dairy group is
a tasty part of MyPlate.
MyPlate is a tool
that helps you eat
healthful food.

DAIRY
On MyPlate

by Mari Schuh
Consulting editor: Gail Saunders-Smith, PhD

Consultant: Barbara J. Rolls, PhD
Guthrie Chair in Nutrition
Pennsylvania State University
University Park, Pennsylvania

CAPSTONE PRESS
a capstone imprint

Pebble Plus is published by Capstone Press,
1710 Roe Crest Drive, North Mankato, Minnesota 56003.
www.capstonepub.com

Library of Congress Cataloging-in-Publication Data
Schuh, Mari C., 1975–
  Dairy on myplate / by Mari Schuh.
    p. cm.—(Pebble plus. What's on myplate?)
  Includes bibliographical references and index.
  Summary: "Simple text and photos describe USDA's MyPlate tool and healthy dairy choices for
children"—Provided by publisher.
  ISBN 978-1-4296-8744-7 (library binding)
  ISBN 978-1-4296-9410-0 (paperback)
  ISBN 978-1-62065-324-1 (eBook PDF)
  ISBN 978-1-4765-3057-4 (e-book)
  1. Dairy products in human nutrition—Juvenile literature. 2. Dairy products-—Juvenile literature. I. Title.

  TX377.S378 2013
  641.3'7—dc23   2012009313

Editorial Credits

Jeni Wittrock, editor; Gene Bentdahl, designer; Svetlana Zhurkin, media researcher; Kathy McColley,
production specialist; Sarah Schuette, photo stylist; Marcy Morin, studio scheduler

Photo Credits

All photos by Capstone Studio/Karon Dubke except:
Shutterstock: Magone, cover (bottom), manaemedia, back cover, Melica, cover (top right); USDA, cover (inset), 5

The author dedicates this book to her niece, Camryn Schuh of Mankato, Minnesota.

Information in this book supports
the U.S. Department of Agriculture's
MyPlate food guidance system found at
www.choosemyplate.gov. Food amounts
listed in this book are based on daily
recommendations for children ages 4-8.
The amounts listed in this book are
appropriate for children who get less than
30 minutes a day of moderate physical
activity, beyond normal daily activities.
Children who are more physically active
may be able to eat more while staying
within calorie needs. The U.S. Department
of Agriculture (USDA) does not endorse
any products, services, or organizations.

Note to Parents and Teachers

The What's on MyPlate? series supports national science standards related to health and
nutrition. This book describes and illustrates MyPlate's dairy recommendations. The images
support early readers in understanding the text. The repetition of words and phrases helps early
readers learn new words. This book also introduces early readers to subject-specific vocabulary
words, which are defined in the Glossary section. Early readers may need assistance to read
some words and to use the Table of Contents, Glossary, Read More, Internet Sites, and Index
sections of the book.

Printed in the United States of America in North Mankato, Minnesota.
122013   007928R

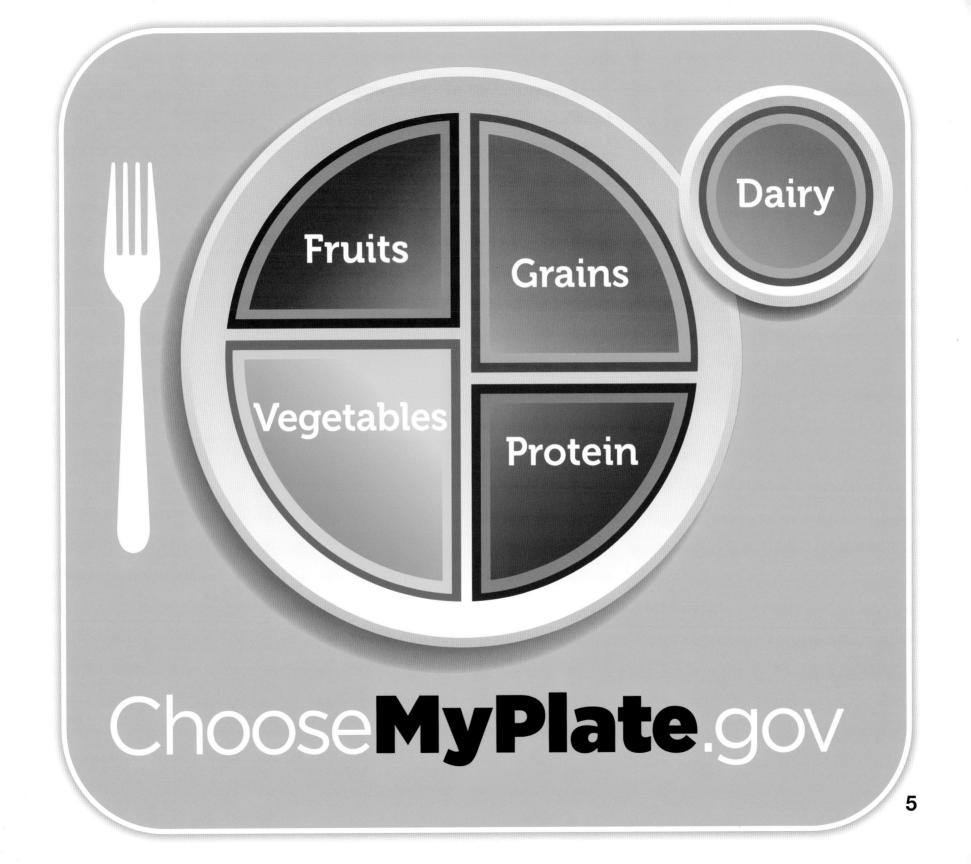

Fruits

Grains

Vegetables

Protein

Dairy

ChooseMyPlate.gov

Dairy Foods

Milk, cheese,
and yogurt are part
of the dairy group.
Have you eaten
dairy foods today?

Dairy foods have calcium.

Your bones and teeth

need calcium

to grow healthy and strong.

Kids ages 4 to 8 should eat and drink 2½ cups (600 milliliters) from the dairy group every day.

Enjoying the Dairy Group

Different kinds of milk have

different amounts of fat.

Choose low-fat milk.

It's better for you.

Cheese can be hard, soft, yellow, or white.

An adult can help you read the labels to choose low-fat cheese.

15

Dairy foods taste great
with other foods.
For a sweet snack,
add fruit to your
creamy yogurt.

Add low-fat yogurt

to your baked potato.

Sprinkle low-fat cheese

on a bowl of soup.

Cream pops are yummy
on a hot afternoon.
What dairy foods
will you choose today?

How Much to Eat

Most kids need to have three servings from the dairy group every day. Pick three of your favorite dairy products to enjoy today!

1/3 cup (80 mL) shredded cheese

1 cup (240 mL) fat-free milk

1½ ounces (45 grams) hard cheese

1 cup (240 mL) pudding made with milk

2 ounces (55 grams) processed cheese

1 cup (240 mL) yogurt

1 cup (240mL) soymilk

2 cups (480 mL) cottage cheese

Glossary

calcium—a mineral that the body uses to build teeth and bones

dairy—foods that are made with milk; milk, cheese, and yogurt are kinds of dairy foods

low-fat—containing a small amount of fat; dairy foods that are low-fat are better for you than dairy foods with more fat

MyPlate—a food plan that reminds people to eat healthful food and be active; MyPlate was created by the U.S. Department of Agriculture

serving—one helping of food

Read More

Borgert-Spaniol, Megan. *Dairy Group.* Eating Right with MyPlate. Minneapolis: Bellwether Media, 2012.

Dilkes, D. H. *Milk and Dairy.* All about Good Foods We Eat. Berkeley Heights, N.J.: Enslow Elementary, 2012.

Lee, Sally. *The Delicious Dairy Group.* First Graphics. MyPlate and Healthy Eating. Mankato, Minn.: Capstone Press, 2012.

Internet Sites

FactHound offers a safe, fun way to find Internet sites related to this book. All of the sites on FactHound have been researched by our staff.

Here's all you do:

Visit *www.facthound.com*

Type in this code: 9781429687447

 Check out projects, games and lots more at
www.capstonekids.com

Index

Word Count: 147
Grade: 1
Early-Intervention Level: 15